In 1935 if you wanted to read a good book, you needed either a lot of money or a library card. Cheap paperbacks were available, but their poor production generally mirrored the quality between the covers. One weekend that year, Allen Lane, Managing Director of The Bodley Head, having spent the weekend visiting Agatha Christie, found himself on a platform at Exeter station trying to find something to read for his journey back to London. He was appalled by the quality of the material he had to choose from. Everything that Allen Lane achieved from that day until his death in 1970 was based on a passionate belief in the existence of 'a vast reading public for *intelligent* books at a low price'. The result of his momentous vision was the birth not only of Penguin, but of the 'paperback revolution'. Quality writing became available for the price of a packet of cigarettes, literature became a mass medium for the first time, a nation of book-borrowers became a nation of book-buyers – and the very concept of book publishing was changed for ever. Those founding principles – of quality and value, with an overarching belief in the fundamental importance of reading – have guided everything the company has done since 1935. Sir Allen Lane's pioneering

at Pe

MORE THAN A BUSINESS

'We decided it was time to end the almost customary half-hearted manner in which cheap editions were produced – as though the only people who could possibly want cheap editions must belong to a lower order of intelligence. We, however, believed in the existence in this country of a vast reading public for intelligent books at a low price, and staked everything on it'
Sir Allen Lane, 1902–1970

'The Penguin Books are splendid value for sixpence, so splendid that if other publishers had any sense they would combine against them and suppress them'
George Orwell

'More than a business ... a national cultural asset'
Guardian

'When you look at the whole Penguin achievement you know that it constitutes, in action, one of the more democratic successes of our recent social history'
Richard Hoggart

Of Pageants and Picnics

ELIZABETH DAVID

PENGUIN BOOKS

PENGUIN BOOKS

Published by the Penguin Group
Penguin Books Ltd, 80 Strand, London WC2R 0RL, England
Penguin Group (USA) Inc., 375 Hudson Street, New York, New York 10014, USA
Penguin Group (Canada), 10 Alcorn Avenue, Toronto, Ontario, Canada M4V 3B2
(a division of Pearson Penguin Canada Inc.)
Penguin Ireland, 25 St Stephen's Green, Dublin 2, Ireland
(a division of Penguin Books Ltd)
Penguin Group (Australia), 250 Camberwell Road, Camberwell, Victoria 3124,
Australia (a division of Pearson Australia Group Pty Ltd)
Penguin Books India Pvt Ltd, 11 Community Centre,
Panchsheel Park, New Delhi – 110 017, India
Penguin Group (NZ), cnr Airborne and Rosedale Roads, Albany,
Auckland 1310, New Zealand (a division of Pearson New Zealand Ltd)
Penguin Books (South Africa) (Pty) Ltd, 24 Sturdee Avenue,
Rosebank 2196, South Africa

Penguin Books Ltd, Registered Offices: 80 Strand, London WC2R 0RL, England

www.penguin.com

Summer Cooking published in Penguin Books 1965

An Omelette and a Glass of Wine published in Penguin Books 1986

South Wind through the Kitchen published in Penguin Books 1998

These extracts published as a Pocket Penguin 2005
1

Set in 11/13pt Monotype Dante
Typeset by Palimpsest Book Production Limited
Polmont, Stirlingshire
Printed in England by Clays Ltd, St Ives plc

Contents

Foreword

All of Elizabeth's friends have stories to tell about her picnics, which ranged between disaster and triumph. Any reason for an outing to a library, gallery, museum or house either in London or further afield was seized upon. When she was writing the bread book a lot of the resources were to be found at the handsome newly built Guildhall Library which opened in October 1974. When the first visit was proposed I asked if she intended to spend just the morning, or the whole day in the library. It was decided that a full day would be required, consulting the catalogue, making notes, ordering books, and so on. Then came the important matter of lunch. Elizabeth telephoned me to say that there was a dearth of anywhere in the City where lunch would be possible. So, a picnic was in order. The formula was of long standing. Elizabeth would bake the bread, bring butter and cheese, fruit and a bottle of wine. My contribution was to cook a Tian in the dish she had given me, according to her perfected recipe, quoted in *Mediterranean Food* from *La Cuisine à Nice* by H. Heyraud.

The next day we set out from Halsey Street in good time and struck lucky. There was a parking place in an extraordinary little square behind the library. The buildings were all high-rise, towering over the square – but to Elizabeth's delight, there in the middle, was a long rectangular pool with varied planting. This included a bushy shrub overhanging the water which was immediately put to use. String was always a vital part of picnic equipment, and so the bottle of white wine was lowered into the pool, and attached to the shrub. That done, we repaired to the library and made a start on the catalogues and the ordering of books. At the end of the morning we returned to the square and set out rugs and cushions, a tablecloth, and then the picnic. Fortunately the wine was still in place, nicely chilled. The sun shone, the food and wine were delicious – useful work accomplished. Altogether a most satisfactory start to a range of similar picnics during that summer of the Guildhall Library run. (And the bottle of wine was always to be found in place.)

April Boyes

Picnics

Picnic addicts seem to be roughly divided between those who frankly make elaborate preparations and leave nothing to chance, and those others whose organization is no less complicated but who are more deceitful and pretend that everything will be obtained on the spot and cooked over a woodcutter's fire, conveniently to hand; there are even those, according to Richard Jefferies, who wisely take the precaution of visiting the site of their intended picnic some days beforehand and there burying the champagne.

Not long before the war I was staying with friends in Marseille. One Saturday night a picnic was arranged for the next day with some American acquaintances; it was agreed that the two parties should proceed in their own cars to a little bay outside Marseille, and that we should each bring our own provisions. On Sunday morning I and my friends indulged in a delicious hour of shopping in the wonderful market of the rue de Rome, buying olives, anchovies, salame sausages, pâtés, yards of bread, smoked fish, fruit and cheese. With a provision of cheap red wine we bundled the food into the car and set off, stopping now and again for a drink; so that we arrived at our rendezvous well disposed to appreciate the sun, the sea and the scent of wild herbs and Mediterranean pines. Presently our friends drove up and started to unload their car. One of the first things to come out was a hatchet, with which they efficiently proceeded to chop down olive branches, and in no time at all there was a blazing fire. Out of their baskets came cutlets, potatoes, bacon, skewers, frying pans, jars of ice, butter, tablecloths, all the trappings of a minor barbecue. Our reactions as we watched these proceedings were those of astonishment, admiration, and finally, as realization of the inadequacy of our own catering dawned, dismay. How wilted they seemed, those little packets wrapped up in rather oily paper; the olives which had glowed with colour in the market stalls of the rue de Rome looked shabby now; the salame seemed dried up and the anchovies a squalid mess. Miserably, like poor relations, we sat with our shameful bundles spread out on the grass and politely offered them to our friends. They were kind, but obviously preferred their own grilled cutlets and fried potatoes, and we were too embarrassed to accept their proffered hospitality. Presently they produced ice cream out of a thermos, but by now we were past caring, and finally it was their turn for surprise when they found we hadn't even provided ourselves with the means of making a cup of coffee.

Then there was the hospitable family I remember in my childhood; they owned a beautiful house and an elegant garden and were much given to out-of-door entertainments, pageants and picnics. On picnic days a large party of children and grown-ups would be assembled in the hall. Led by our host and hostess we proceeded through the exquisite formal Dutch garden, across the lane and over a fence into a coppice. Close on our heels followed the butler, the chauffeur and the footman, bearing fine china plates, the silver and tablecloths, and a number of vast dishes containing cold chickens, jellies and trifles. Arrived at the end of our journey, five minutes from the house, our host set about making a fire, with sticks which I suspect had been strategically placed by the gardener, over which we grilled quantities of sausages and bacon, which were devoured amidst the customary jokes and hilarity. The picnickers' honour thus satisfied, we took our places for an orderly meal, handed round by the footman, and in composition resembling that of an Edwardian wedding breakfast.

Since those days I have had a good many opportunities of evolving a picnic technique on the lines laid down by Henry James, 'not so good as to fail of an amusing disorder, nor yet so bad as to defeat the proper function of repasts'.

Before deciding upon the food, its packing and transport must be planned. (I am assuming for the moment a car-transported picnic.) Those who are lucky enough to possess an Edwardian picnic hamper, fitted with spirit lamp and kettle, sandwich tins and a variety of boxes and bottles, need look no further. These hampers may be cumbersome, but they are capacious and solid; an aura of lavish gallivantings and ancient Rolls-Royces hangs about them, and they are infinitely superior to the modern kind in which the use of every inch of space has been planned for you in advance. (At the Lord Roberts workshop in the Brompton Road there are deep square baskets of very solid construction, large enough to hold a good deal of food as well as several bottles, which are still very reasonable in price. This establishment is full of happy ideas for all addicts of eating out of doors, for they sell large hampers, unfitted, so that you can pack whatever you please, baskets with divisions for bottles, baskets for thermos jars, and the most comfortable garden chairs in existence.) Insulated picnic bags are highly effective and useful.

As to plates and glasses, if I am going to have them at all I would prefer to have china plates and glass glasses, although it must be admitted that clear, colourless plastic glasses such as are used on airlines are more practical.

A spirit lamp and kettle plus a tin of Nescafé provide a hotter and fresher cup of coffee than any which ever came out of a vacuum flask. Iced coffee on the other hand can be transported in thermos jugs, and a large thermos jar filled with ice is a blessing for those who don't care for warm drinks, or who like to put ice into coarse red picnic wine.

As for the food, the buying and preparing of it always seem to me to provide half the fun. The possibilities are almost without limit. On the whole, though, I think that such elegant foods as foie gras and lobster patties should be excluded as they seem to lose their fine lustre when eaten out of doors, whereas the simpler charms of salame sausage, fresh cheese, black olives and good French bread (if you can find such a commodity) are enhanced when they are eaten on the hillside or the seashore. Sandwiches I rather like (George Saintsbury considered that venison makes the best sandwiches), but many people do not, so there must always be alternatives; thin slices of ham rolled round Frankfurter sausages, or Frankfurter sausages split in half enclosing a slice of Gruyère cheese are good ones. Remember that such delicious foods as jellied egg, duck in aspic, and so on aren't really ideal for long journeys on a hot day because the jelly (if it has been made as it should be) will melt *en route*; mayonnaise also has a dismaying habit of turning into a rather unappetizing-looking oily mass when the weather is hot. A cold chicken with a cream sauce is a better bid than a chicken mayonnaise. Cold steak and kidney pudding is fine picnic food, so is cold spiced beef, which cuts into nice slices. Cold escalopes of veal, fried in egg and breadcrumbs, make excellent picnic food provided they are very thin and very well drained after frying. Hard-boiled eggs are time-honoured picnic food, so I always take a few, but they are not everybody's taste. Cheese seems to me essential for an out-of-doors meal; next to the salty little Mediterranean goat and sheep's milk cheeses English Cheddar or Cheshire, or Gruyère, are perhaps the easiest picnic cheeses. Some people like a rich moist fruit cake for a picnic, but I prefer a slab of the dryest, bitterest chocolate available (Terry's make a good one but the best is the Belgian Côte d'Or), to be eaten in alternate mouthfuls with a Marie biscuit. Apples and figs and apricots, because they are easy to eat and transport as well as being good in the open air, are perhaps the best fruit for a picnic.

The nicest drinks for picnics are the obvious ones. A stout red wine such as a Macon or a Chianti, which cannot be unduly harmed by the journey in the car; vin rosé (particularly delicious by the sea); cider, lager, shandy, Black Velvet; iced sherry and bitters. For a very hot day Pimm's No. 1 couldn't be bettered but involves some organization in the matter of cucumber, lemonade, oranges, mint, borage, and all the paraphernalia, and a thermos jar of ice is essential. An effective way to keep wine and mineral waters cool on a long journey is to wrap the bottles in several sheets of dampened newspaper.

For soft drinks the most refreshing are tinned grapefruit, orange or pineapple juice, and tomato juice. (In this case include the tin opener.) Delicate china tea, iced, with slices of lemon and mint leaves is admirably reviving. An early edition of Mrs Beeton asserts that 'Water can usually be obtained so it is useless to take it'. For the walker's picnic perhaps the perfect meal has been described by Sir Osbert Sitwell: 'the fruits of the month, cheese with the goaty taste of mountains upon it, and if possible bilberries, apples, raw celery, a meal unsophisticated and pastoral . . .'.

SMOKED TROUT OR SMOKED MACKEREL SANDWICHES

Fillet the trout or mackerel (smoked mackerel, although not so well known, are cheaper than smoked trout, and excellent), spread buttered rye bread with a layer of horseradish cream and place the fillets of fish on top.

BACON AND LETTUCE SANDWICHES

One cos lettuce; one large rasher of bacon for each round of sandwiches; a mustardy French dressing. Shred the lettuce fairly fine and toss it in the dressing without letting it get sodden. Cut each rasher of bacon in half and fry very lightly. Put a layer of lettuce on the buttered bread and the bacon on top.

SHOOTER'S SANDWICH

'The wise, "at least among the children of this world", to use one of Walter Pater's careful qualifying phrases, travel with a flask of whisky-and-water and what I call a "Shooter's Sandwich". This last is made thus: Take a large, thick, excellent rump steak. Do not season it, for that would cause the juice to run out, and in grilling it keep it markedly underdone. Have ready a sandwich loaf one end of which has been cut off and an adequate portion of the contents of which has been removed. Put the steak, hot from the grill, and – but only then – somewhat highly seasoned, into the loaf; add a few grilled mushrooms; replace the deleted end of the loaf; wrap the loaf in a double sheet of clean white blotting-paper, tie with twine both ways, superimpose a sheet of grease-proof paper, and more twine. Place a moderate weight on top, and after a while add other weights. Let the thing endure pressure for at least six hours. Do not carve it until and as each slice is required.

'With this "sandwich" a man may travel from Land's End to Quaker Oats, and snap his fingers at both.'

T. Earle Welby, *The Dinner Knell*, Methuen, 1932

I have sometimes made this sandwich and kept it in the refrigerator as an emergency store when packing, moving house, and at other times when, although too busy to cook, everyone needs good nourishing food. For such occasions, as well as for picnics and journeys, T. Earle Welby's recipe is invaluable.

FRENCH GARLIC LOAVES

Heat a couple of French loaves a few minutes in the oven. While they are still hot, split them lengthwise and spread each side with butter into which you have pounded one clove of garlic, some chopped parsley and a little salt. Put the two halves together, and when you get to the picnic cut them into slices in the ordinary way.

PRAWNS WITH WATERCRESS DRESSING

For a seaside picnic it is nice to have some fish; in all probability you won't find it there, so take it with you. Buy the ready peeled prawns, put them into a suitable jar, season with salt and pepper, and take in a separate bottle a generous quantity of French dressing made with lemon juice instead of vinegar, into which you mix a good handful of very finely chopped watercress.

COLD SPICED SALT BEEF

Soak a piece of salted silverside in warm water for half an hour. Make about a dozen incisions all round the beef into which you insert half cloves of garlic rolled in chopped fresh herbs; rub it all over with ground cloves and ground black pepper and put it into a pan with half a glass of red wine, enough water to cover, and thyme, bayleaves, marjoram, rosemary and an onion. Bring it to the boil, then cover it closely and put it in a low oven until it is tender – about 1 hour and 20 minutes for two pounds of beef: but as the quality of salt beef varies considerably it is advisable to try it from time to time, for if it is over-cooked it will crumble to pieces when cut.

When it is done, take it out of the pan and put it on a board, cover it with a piece of grease-proof paper and put a weight on it. Next day it can be cut into fine slices.

FIGS AND CREAM CHEESE

Dried figs are delicious for a picnic; agreeable to bite on at the end of a meal. Have with them a home-made sour milk cheese, very slightly salted, or little French cream cheeses.

ORIENTAL PICNICS

1

'When I was going through the course of Garrison instruction, and accustomed to long days out surveying, I was partial to a galantine made of a small fowl, boned and rolled, with a block of tongue and some forcemeat introduced into the centre of it. A home-made brawn of tongue, a part of an ox-head, and sheep's trotters, well seasoned, and slightly spiced, was another specialité.

'A nice piece of the brisket of beef salted and spiced, boiled, placed under a weight, and then trimmed into a neat shape is a very handy thing for the tiffin basket; and a much respected patron of mine recommends for travelling, a really good cold plum pudding in which a glass of brandy has been included.'

2

'The traveller's luncheon basket, and that of the sportsman are analogous. A friend of mine with whom I used to walk the paddy fields adopted the plan of taking out a digester pot, previously filled with stewed steak and oysters, or some equally toothsome stew. This he trusted to his syce, who lit a fire somewhere or other, in the marvellous way the natives of this country do, and, as sure as there are fish in the sea, had the contents of the pot steaming hot, at the exact spot, and at the very moment we required it.'

Extracts from *Culinary Jottings for Madras,*
'Wyvern' (Col. Kenney Herbert,) 1885

3

Charles Baskerville, the American painter, has described an Indian picnic given by the Maharajah of Jaipur, in 1937.

'Yesterday we spent the whole day picnicking . . . a lorry with lunch and bottles followed our car . . . one thing I particularly like about these outdoor luncheons is the cold fried fish. Besides the European food there are always some spicy Indian dishes . . . cold curry of boars' head (without the eyes) or peppery leaves of spinach fried in batter . . . of course a hamper of whisky, beer, gimlets, cider, and water is always taken along.'

4

My own experience of Indian picnics wasn't always quite so satisfactory. There was one in particular, a moonlight picnic near the Kutub Minar, the leaning tower near Delhi. There was nothing wrong with the transport, the food, or the moonlight; we had merely reckoned without the hordes of half wild dogs which are a familiar feature of Indian outdoor life. Scarcely had we time to draw the cork of a bottle of the Rhinegold Australian hock which we were lucky to get in war-time India than we were surrounded by nearly every dog in the province; literally surrounded. They did not apparently want food, or at any rate not our food; they simply formed a circle round us at a respectful distance and stared and howled.

First we pretended not to notice, then we shoo-ed them away several times. They returned immediately, with reinforcements, re-formed their dreadful circle, and howled and stared and sniffed again, until they forced us to get into our cars and return to the city, leaving them in possession of their ruin.

5

In Egypt the picnic season starts sometimes in March, with *Shem el Nessim*, the 'smelling of the Zephyrs', a day which is kept as a public holiday, when the whole population goes out to eat in the open air and greet the first day of Spring.

An agreeable form of picnic in Cairo was the felucca party; on board a hired Nile sailing boat Arab servants would carry the food; there were copper trays of pimentos, small marrows and vine leaves stuffed with rice, large, round shallow metal dishes filled with meat and spiced pilaff, bowls of grapes and peaches and figs and melons cooled with lumps of ice, mounds of flat Arab loaves stuffed with a salad of tomatoes, onions and mint; there would be music and the wailing of Arab songs as the boat swung rather wildly about, the crew made Turkish coffee, and we drank the odd, slightly salty red Egyptian wine from the Mariut, one of the oldest wine-producing regions in the world.

Eating Out in Provincial France

Picnics in France combine so many joys. First, the buying, to be done as often as possible in a market rather than in shops. At the stalls there is more choice, the produce is fresher and cheaper, buying is quicker, there is the chance of talking to the local people, of finding the country women who have brought in a basket of fresh cheeses, unsalted farm butter, perhaps a few bunches of sorrel, some garden radishes. There is the stimulus of seeing the abundance of produce and its magnificent quality. There is also, unless you are staying in the country on a self-catering basis, the frustration of not being able to take armfuls of it home to cook for yourself. And yet again it must be asked why do the restaurants nowadays so seldom offer a dish of fresh vegetables on their menus? What has become of the homely vegetable soup which used to appear nightly on all country restaurant and hotel menus?

Now, for the pleasure of buying bread. I look, usually, for a bakery selling the big round loaves called *miches* or *boules* or just *pains de campagne*. Those have more character, a more interesting flavour and stay fresher much longer than *baguettes* and *ficelles* and all the rest of the tribe of long loaves. Enticing though these look and smell as they come out of the oven, I find them lacking in savour, although they certainly still compare pretty well with the factory bread which is our own national shame.

When lunchtime approaches, the question is are we near a river or lake? If so, shall we be able to reach its banks? For the ideal picnic there has to be water, and from that point of view, France is wonderful picnic country, so rich in magnificent rivers, waterfalls, reservoirs, that it is rare not to be able to find some delicious spot where you can sit by the water, watch dragonflies and listen to the birds or to the beguiling sound of a fast-flowing stream. As you drink wine from a tumbler, sprinkle your bread with olive oil and salt, and eat it with ripe tomatoes or rough country sausage you feel better off than in even the most perfect restaurant. During one golden September in the valleys of the Corrèze, the Dordogne and the Lot, I enjoyed just such picnics, day after blazing day. The tomatoes that year and in that region were so rich and ripe and fragrant that I shall forever remember their savour. Then, one day in a pastry shop in Beaulieu-sur-Dordogne, we bought a *tarte aux mirabelles* made with yeast pastry. Those little round golden plums of early autumn on their light brioche-like base made an unexpected and memorable end to our outdoor feast. Another year it was Normandy, early autumn again, and daily picnics in the magnificent forests of Mortagne, Brotonne and Bellême, in clearings where foxgloves grew high amid the bracken, and water was always within sight. Once or twice we sat by the banks of the Seine, looking at landscapes and riverscapes which Corot had surely painted.

The Markets of France

Cavaillon

It is a Sunday evening in mid-June. The cafés of Cavaillon are crammed. There isn't an inch to park your car. The noise is tremendous. In the most possible of the hotels – it goes by the name of Toppin – all the rooms are taken by seven o'clock. But the little Auberge La Provençale in the rue Chabran is quite quiet and you can enjoy a good little dinner – nothing spectacular, but genuine and decently cooked food well served – and go to bed early. The chances are you won't sleep much though, because Monday is the big market day in Cavaillon and soon after midnight the carts and lorries and vans of the big fruit farmers' co-operatives, of the market gardeners, of the tomato and garlic and onion growers, will start rattling and roaring and rumbling into the great open market in the place du Clos.

At dawn they will be unloading their melons and asparagus, their strawberries and red currants and cherries, their apricots and peaches and pears and plums, their green almonds, beans, lettuces, shining new white onions, new potatoes, vast bunches of garlic. By six o'clock the ground will be covered with *cageots*, the chip vegetable and fruit baskets, making a sea of soft colours and shadowy shapes in the dawn light. The air of the Place is filled with the musky scent of those little early Cavaillon melons, and then you become aware of another powerfully conflicting smell – rich, clove-like, spicy. It is the scent of sweet basil, and it is coming from the far end of the market where a solitary wrinkled old man sits on an upturned basket, scores and scores of basil plants ringed all around him like a protective hedge. With a beady eye he watches the drama of the market place. The dealers, exporters and wholesalers walking round inspecting the produce, discussing prices, negotiating; the hangers-on standing about in groups smoking, chatting; the market police and official inspectors strolling round seeing that all is in order.

On the whole the scene is quiet, quieter at least than you would expect considering that this is one of the most important wholesale fruit and vegetable markets in France, the great distributing centre for the *primeurs* of the astonishingly fertile and productive areas of the Vaucluse and the Comtat Venaissin – areas which less than a hundred years ago were desperately poor, inadequately irrigated, isolated for lack of roads and transport, earthquake-stricken, devastated by blights which destroyed the cereal crops and the vines.

But now seven o'clock strikes in the market at Cavaillon. The lull is over. This is the moment when the goods change hands. Pandemonium breaks loose. The dealers snatch the baskets of produce they have bought and rush them to waiting lorries. A cartload of garlic vanishes from under your nose. A mountain of melons evaporates in a wink. If you try to speak to anybody you will be ignored, if you get in the way you'll be knocked down in the wild scramble to get goods away to Paris, London, Brussels, and all the great centres of northern and eastern France. Suddenly, the market place is deserted.

At eight o'clock you emerge from the café where you have had your breakfast coffee and croissant. The market place is, to put it mildly, astir once more. It is surrounded by vans and lorries disgorging cheap dresses and overalls, plastic kitchenware, shoes and scarves and bales of cotton, piles of plates and jugs, nails and screws and knives, farm implements and packets of seeds, cartons of dried-up-looking biscuits and trays of chemically-coloured sweets.

You dive down a side street where you have spied a festoon of pretty cotton squares, and there, under gaudy painted colonnades, lilac and orange, cinnamon and lemon and rose, in patterns more typical of Marseille or the Levant than of Cavaillon, the retail market stalls are already doing business. The displays seem rather tame after the wholesale market and there is not a melon to be seen. It is too early in the season, they are still too expensive for the housewives of Cavaillon. Five thousand francs a kilo they were fetching today, and a week later in London shops 12s. 6d. each for little tiny ones. But the street opposite the painted colonnades leads into the square where more and more food stalls are opening and the housewives are already busy marketing. Here you can buy everything for a picnic lunch. Beautiful sprawling ripe tomatoes, a Banon cheese wrapped in chestnut leaves, Arles sausages, pâté, black olives, butter cut from a towering monolith, apricots, cherries.

It is still early and you can drive out towards Apt and branch off across the Lubéron. The roads are sinuous but almost empty, and they will take you through some of the most beautiful country in Provence. Perched on the hillsides are typical old Provençal villages, some, like Oppède-le-Vieux, crumbling, haunted, half-deserted, others like Bonnieux with a flourishing modern village built below the old one, and up beyond Apt, through the dramatic stretch of ochre-mining country, the strange red-gold village of Roussillon appears to be toppling precariously on the edge of a craggy cliff. Round about here, the network of caves under the ochreous rocks has been turned into vast *champignonnières*, and at the modest little Restaurant David (no relation) you can eat the local cultivated mushrooms cooked *à la crème* or *à la provençale* with, naturally, olive oil, parsley and garlic. And the Rose d'Or, a little hotel opened only a few weeks ago, promises a welcome alternative to the establishments of Apt, Aix and Cavaillon.

Yvetot

Duclair is a little town on a loop of the Seine twenty kilometres outside Rouen towards Dieppe. It is not particularly picturesque and the main road and the ferry over the Seine make it noisy. But I always try to stay the night there on my way down through France and on the way back again because of the Hôtel de la Poste where the Swiss proprietor and his pretty Norman wife provide such a warm welcome and such good food. Their big airy dining-room overlooks the river, their delicious pâté of Rouen duckling cooked with port is brought to table in the gigantic old terrines in which it has been baked, their hors-d'œuvres are always fresh, well chosen, original and beautifully served, ducks and chickens are roasted on a spit in the old Norman fireplace in the kitchen.

And if you happen to arrive on a Monday evening you could see a typical Norman market, both wholesale and retail, at Duclair early on Tuesday morning. It is as good a way as any to the beginnings of an understanding and appreciation of any French province, to see the local markets in action, to watch the produce unloaded from the carts and vans, to hear the talk of the farmers and buyers in the cafés after the main business has been transacted. And to us, whose country markets are rapidly vanishing, the extraordinary activity and the variety of foodstuffs on sale in a little town of only three thousands inhabitants like Duclair, so few miles away from Dover, has a particular fascination.

One could almost go over there to do one's weekly marketing – or on into Rouen, where the big market day is also on Tuesday, and from where you could bring home butter made from unpasteurized cream, great bowls of *tripes à la mode*, and duck pâtés, and baskets full of big round Breton artichokes for a tenth of the price we have to pay here. And Norman cheeses too: genuine Pont-l'Evèque made on the farms of the Pays d'Auge from milk still warm from the cows; Livarot, that powerful and marvellous cheese which has been made in the district since the thirteenth century; even a good Norman Camembert can be found if you look. But progress is on the march in Normandy, and in a big way. It won't be long before cheeses such as these become rarities. More and more of the farms are going over to pasteurized milk, their produce is sent to the co-operatives, the butter and the cheese no longer have the characteristic ripe flavours one used to expect. On the whole, though, the Norman producers are acting with sense and foresight over the development of their dairy industry. They are frankly calling their new cheeses by new brand names, making them in different shapes and original packings, selling them on their own merits rather than attempting to pass them off as the great traditional products of an unmechanized and unstandardized age.

There are, of course, big areas of Normandy where the farmers are still producing milk, butter, cream and cheeses by the old methods. The outlets for these products are the local wholesale markets.

The great centre of the rich Pays d'Auge, also cider and Calvados country, is Vimoutiers, only a few kilometres from the cheese villages of both Camembert and Livarot. The big butter market is on Monday afternoons. The centre of the Bray district is Gournay, where over a hundred years ago Petit Suisse cream cheeses were evolved by a farmer's wife and a Swiss herdsman. There are now almost a dozen different varieties of these cream cheeses, and the Gervais factory, at Ferrières, absorbs something like 50,000 gallons of milk daily for the demi-sel and other fresh cheeses.

Yvetot is the great butter market of the Caux country and provides a sight worth seeing if you happen to be in the district on a Wednesday morning. Out of the vans are coming huge cones of butter fresh from the farms. It is made from ripened, unpasteurized cream, and divided into loaves of 35 or 70 kilos each; they are wrapped in crisp white cloths or in polythene wrappings and stacked in huge baskets or wire carriers. Each parcel of butter is tasted with a long scoop and then re-weighed before a buyer will accept it. On the long rows of stalls are ranged all sorts of fresh farm products – eggs, vegetables, salads, churns of cream, live chickens and ducks – brown Rouen ducks, black Muscovy ducks, white Pekin ducks, turkeys, baby chicks; one old woman has just one basket of produce for sale – eggs, a few fresh peas, and a bunch of green turnip-tops. But even this little collection of cottage garden produce won't change hands without some stern bargaining.

As for the farm butter, it is being borne away by the purchasers in the great baskets which look as if they might have been used by the Scarlet Pimpernel to smuggle refugee *aristos* out of Paris. Tomorrow this butter will be enriching many a roast chicken, thousands of omelettes and cakes and pastries, filling the kitchens of France with the incomparable scent of butter gently sizzling in a frying pan . . .

And indeed it is high time to think about lunch. There is Tôtes not far away on the Dieppe road, and the famous old Hôtel des Cygnes where Guy de Maupassant wrote *Boule de Suif* and where the proprietor appears the very embodiment of Norman robustness. At the Marée in the market place of Rouen there are delicious fish dishes, excellent food at the Beffroy in the rue du Beffroy, all the more unexpected because the place looks too like Ye Olde Bunne Shoppe to be true. But perhaps it is better to avoid Rouen, the midday traffic going in and coming out is too much of a worry. Better to drive a bit farther, down into lower Normandy and the beautiful Vallée d'Auge, past old Norman farms and manors, through country thick with apple trees, and pastures so opulent and green that unless you have seen some of the raw, rebuilt little towns, it is hard to believe in the terrible devastation of only fifteen years ago.

At Orbec, twenty kilometres from Lisieux, is the Caneton, a restaurant which you know is going to be good as soon as you enter its doors – the smell is so appetizing – but it is small and not exactly unknown, so it is prudent to telephone for a table in advance. The *menu gastronomique* at the Caneton is generous and good value for 1800 francs, but a trifle fussy and rich, and a better choice for my taste is the *plat du jour*, with perhaps a duck liver pâté, or local *charcuterie*, to start with, which is what you see the inhabitants eating.

Montpellier

'Buy a pound of choucroûte from a village charcutier. As you pass the municipal pump, pause a moment . . .'

Any English cookery writer who published a recipe opening with these words would be thought distinctly out of touch. The evocative sentence comes in fact from a little book called *La Cuisine en Plein Air* by that most adorable of French gastronomes, Dr Edouard de Pomiane. The little volume, which deals with cooking out of doors for motorists, cyclists, campers, walkers, and fishermen has never been translated into English and wouldn't be of much practical use to us if it were, because the majority of the recipes are based on the products to be bought at the 'village *charcutier*', an institution which doesn't exist in the British Isles.

It is only when one has haunted the markets of

France and the food shops in the country towns and villages, watched the housewives doing their shopping, listened to them discussing their purchases at the *pâtisseries* and the *charcuteries* that one realizes how much less they are tied to their kitchens than we had always been led to suppose.

The point is that in France no shame is attached to buying ready-prepared food because most of it is of high quality. The housewives and small restaurateurs who rely upon the professional skill of *charcutiers* and *pâtissiers* for a part of their supplies see to it that the pâtés and sausages, the little salads for hors-d'œuvre, the galantines and terrines and fish quenelles, the hams and tongues and pies, pastries and fruit flans, the petits fours and the croissants maintain high standards of freshness and excellence, and that any popular regional speciality of the district continues to be cooked with the right and proper traditional ingredients, even if the methods have been speeded up by the introduction of modern machinery.

Here in England we find little in our local delicatessen shop – the only approximation we have to the *charcutier* who sells many ready-prepared foods besides pork butchers' products – but mass-produced sausages, pork pies and fish cakes off a conveyor belt, piled slices of pale pink and blood-red flannel which pass respectively for cooked ham and tongue, bottles of pickled onions and jars of red cabbage in vinegar, possibly a potato salad dressed with synthetic mayonnaise and, with luck, some herrings in brine. In any French town of any size at all we find perhaps three or four rival *charcutiers* displaying trays of shining olives, black and green, large and small, pickled gherkins, capers, home-made mayonnaise, grated carrot salad, shredded celeriac in *rémoulade* sauce, several sorts of tomato salad, sweet-sour onions, *champignons à la Grecque*, ox or pig's muzzle finely sliced and dressed with a vinaigrette sauce and fresh parsley, a salad of mussels, another of cervelas sausage; several kinds of pork pâté; sausages for grilling, sausages for boiling, sausages for hors-d'œuvre, flat sausages called *crépinettes* for baking or frying, salt pork to enrich stews and soups and vegetable dishes, pigs' trotters ready cooked and breadcrumbed, so that all you need to do is to take them home and grill them; cooked ham, raw ham, a galantine of tongue, cold pork and veal roasts, boned stuffed ducks and chickens . . . So it isn't difficult for the housewife in a hurry to buy a little selection, however modest, of these things from the *charcuterie*, and plus her own imagination and something she has perhaps already in the larder to serve an appetizing and fresh little mixed hors-d'œuvre.

When we visited the big open-air retail market in the upper town at Montpellier, there was an ordinary enough little *charcuterie-épicerie* stall offering the ingredients of what might be called the small change of French cookery, but to our English eyes it looked particularly inviting and interesting.

The atmosphere helped, of course. The sun, the clear sky, the bright colours, the prosperous look of this lively, airy university town and wine-growing capital; the stalls massed with flowers; fresh fish shining pink and gold and silver in shallow baskets; cherries and apricots and peaches on the fruit barrows; one stall piled with about a ton of little bunches of soup or pot-au-feu vegetables – a couple of slim leeks, a carrot or two, a long thin turnip, celery leaves, and parsley, all cleaned and neatly bound with a rush, ready for the pot; another *charcuterie* stall, in the covered part of the market, displaying yards of fresh sausage festooned around a pyramid-shaped wire stand; a fishwife crying pussy's parcels of fish wrapped tidily in newspaper; an old woman at the marked entrance selling winkles from a little cart shaped like a pram; a fastidiously dressed old gentleman choosing tomatoes and leaf artichokes, one by one, as if he were picking a bouquet of flowers, and taking them to the scales to be weighed (how extraordinary that we in England put up so docilely with not being permitted by greengrocers or even barrow boys to touch or smell the produce we are buying); a lorry with an old upright piano in the back threading round and round the market place trying to get out. These little scenes establish the character of Montpellier market in our memories, although by now we have spent many mornings in different southern markets and have become accustomed to the beauty and profusion of the produce for sale and to the heavy smell of fresh ripe fruit which everywhere hangs thick in the air at this time of year.

Well, plenty of tourists spend their mornings in museums and picture galleries and cathedrals, and nobody would quarrel with them for that. But the stomach of a city is also not without its importance. And then, I wouldn't be too sure that the food market of a big city shouldn't be counted as part of its artistic tradition.

Where do they get their astonishing gifts for display,

these French stall keepers? Why does a barrow boy selling bunched radishes and salad greens in the market at Chinon know by instinct so to arrange his produce that he has created a little spectacle as fresh and gay as a Dufy painting, and you are at once convinced that unless you taste some of his radishes you will be missing an experience which seems of more urgency than a visit to the Château of Chinon? How has a Montpellier fishwife so mastered the art of composition that with her basket of fish for the *bouillabaisse* she is presenting a picture of such splendour that instead of going to look at the famous collection of paintings in the Musée Fabre you drive off as fast as possible to the coast to order a dish cooked with just such fish? And what can there be about the arrangement of a few slices of sausage and a dozen black olives on a dish brought by the waitress in the seaside café to keep you occupied while your fish is cooking that makes you feel that this is the first time you have seen and tasted a black olive and a piece of sausage?

When one tries to analyse the real reasons for the respect which French cookery has so long exacted from the rest of the world, the French genius for presentation must be counted as a very relevant point, and its humble beginnings can be seen on the market stalls, in the small town *charcutiers'* and *pâtissiers'* shops, in the modest little restaurants where even if the cooking is not particularly distinguished, the most ordinary of little dishes will be brought to your table with respect, properly arranged on a serving dish, the vegetables separately served, the object of arousing your appetite will be achieved and the proprietors of the establishment will have made the most of their limited resources.

This in a sense is the exact reverse of English practice. We seem to exert every effort to make the least of the most. When you order a grilled Dover sole in an English restaurant it will very likely be a fine sole, fresh and well cooked. But when it is dumped unceremoniously before you with a mound of inappropriate green peas and a pool of cold tartare sauce spreading beside it on the hot plate, then your appetite begins to seep away . . .

To decorate a dish of smoked salmon, so beautiful in itself, with lettuce leaves, or to strew it with tufts of cress, is not to make that salmon which has cost 38s. a pound look as if it cost £3, but to belittle it so that you begin to feel it is some bargain basement left-over which needs to be disguised. Alas, where here is our celebrated capacity for understatement? Well, we have our own gifts, but the presentation of food is not one of them, and since French cooks and food purveyors so often appear to lose the lightness of their touch in this respect when they leave their native land and settle abroad, one can only conclude that the special stimulant which brings these gifts into flower is in the air of France itself. Does it sound trivial or over-rarefied to make so much of such small points? I don't think anyone in full possession of their five senses would find it so.

Writing of the work of Chardin, whose most profoundly moving paintings are revelations of how trivial, homely, everyday scenes and objects are transformed for us when we see them through the eyes of a great painter, Proust says, 'Chardin has taught us that a pear is as living as a woman, a kitchen crock as beautiful as an emerald.' Since Proust wrote these words painters and writers have revealed other beauties to us – they have made us see the poetry of factory canteens and metro stations, the romance of cog-wheels, iron girders, bombed buildings, dustbins and pylons. But in the excitement of discovering these wondrous things we shall be poorer if we don't also give a thought now and again to the pear and the kitchen crock.

Valence

To drive from Lascaux of the prehistoric caves in the Dordogne right across country to Valence on the Rhône is possibly not the most expeditious way of getting from the deep south-west of France to the Mediterranean. But if time is not too desperately important it is one way of seeing a vast stretch of surprising and magnificent country, some interesting and unspoiled old towns, perhaps even of discovering some village in the heart of the still primitive agricultural Auvergne, some little-known hotel where one would like to stay instead of hurrying on, to which one would return another year. At the least, perhaps a country inn somewhere in the Limousin or the Cantal district will yield a new dish or a wine which was worth the détour. A *charcuterie* in Aurillac or Vic-sur-Cère or some other small but locally important town will possibly provide a pâté the like of which you never tasted before, or a locally cured ham, a few slices of which you will buy and carry away with a salad, a kilo of peaches, a bottle of Monbazillac and a baton of bread, and somewhere on a hillside amid the mile upon mile of golden broom or close to a splashing waterfall you will have, just for once, the ideal picnic.

Was it up here above Aurillac that one of our party found the best picnic place in France? A stretch of water, mysterious, still, full of plants and birds, away from the road, sheltered with silver birches, and with a stone table evidently waiting there especially for us?

We had driven from Montignac near Lascaux. We had stayed at the Soleil d'Or, a little hotel as warm-hearted as its name. We had eaten a good dinner – among other things a golden bolster of an omelette bursting its seams with truffles – and drunk some excellent red wine of Cahors and afterwards a glass of that remarkable *eau-de-vie* of plums called *Vieille Prune* which is one of the great Dordogne products – another is the odd and delicious walnut oil with which, if you are lucky, you may get your salad dressed.

In spite of all this, or perhaps because of it, we made an early enough start to reach Aurillac in plenty of time to buy our picnic lunch and see something of the old town. Had it been a Saturday we should have stayed to see the cheese market. For Aurillac is one of the centres for the distribution of the splendid cheese of Cantal, to my mind one of the best and most interesting in France. It is a cheese which has a texture not unlike a good Lancashire, and when properly matured a flavour which beats most modern English cheeses on their own ground. There is also a less interesting, creamy, unripened version called a *tomme de Cantal*, much used for cooking, especially in farmhouse potato and egg dishes.

After our picnic lunch we'll have to hurry. We must get across the Plomb du Cantal, into the Velay, and through the scruffy pilgrimage town of Le Puy. But I shall stop to buy some of those beautiful little slate-green lentils for which the district is famous and which a greedy guest of mine recently proclaimed as good as caviare – and also to telephone to Madame Barattero at the Hôtel du Midi at Lamastre to say we are coming for dinner.

Italian Fish Markets

Of all the spectacular food markets in Italy, the one near the Rialto in Venice must be the most remarkable. The light of a Venetian dawn in early summer – you must be about at four o'clock in the morning to see the market coming to life – is so limpid and so still that it makes every separate vegetable and fruit and fish luminous with a life of its own, with unnaturally heightened colours and clear stencilled outlines. Here the cabbages are cobalt blue, the beetroots deep rose, the lettuces clear pure green, sharp as glass. Bunches of gaudy gold marrow-flowers show off the elegance of pink and white marbled bean pods, primrose potatoes, green plums, green peas. The colours of the peaches, cherries and apricots, packed in boxes lined with sugar-bag blue paper matching the blue canvas trousers worn by the men unloading the gondolas, are reflected in the rose-red mullet and the orange *vongole* and *cannestrelle* which have been prised out of their shells and heaped into baskets. In other markets, on other shores, the unfamiliar fishes may be livid, mysterious, repellent, fascinating, and bright with splendid colour; only in Venice do they look good enough to eat. In Venice even ordinary sole and ugly great skate are striped with delicate lilac lights, the sardines shine like newly-minted silver coins, pink Venetian *scampi* are fat and fresh, infinitely enticing in the early dawn.

The gentle swaying of the laden gondolas, the

movements of the market men as they unload, swinging the boxes and baskets ashore, the robust life and rattling noise contrasted with the fragile taffeta colours and the opal sky of Venice – the whole scene is out of some marvellous unheard-of ballet.

A very different kettle of fish, indeed, is the market of Genoa. Nothing will shake my conviction that Genova *la superba* is the noisiest city on earth. (This is nothing new; travellers have constantly remarked upon the fact.) The market-place will therefore be quite a rest; here one is oblivious of the uproar, spellbound by the spectacle of the odd fish which come up from these waters. Their names are descriptive enough: the angler or frogfish, the praying-fish, the sea-hen, the scorpion, the sea-cat, the sea-date, the sea-truffle, sea-snails, sea-strawberries, and a mussel with a hair-covered shell called *cozze pelose*. No wonder that anybody with a spark of imagination is prepared to put up with the ear-splitting din of Genoa, the crashing of trams and trains, the screeching of brakes, and even the agonized wailing of itinerant musicians in the taverns, in order to taste some of these sea beasts when they have been converted into *burrida*, the Genoese fish stew, or into the immense edifice of crustaceans, molluscs, fish, vegetables, and green sauce, which is known as *cappon magro*.

Along the coast at Santa Margherita the fish market is famous; here the fish are less forbidding and savage of aspect, but their brilliance of colour is phenomenal. Huge baskets are filled with what from a distance one takes to be strawberries but which turn out to be huge prawns (they are scarlet by nature, before they are cooked); dark green and grey *tonnetto*, gleaming silver with phosphorescence, are thrust head downwards, like so many French loaves, in a high basket; *moscardini*, brown and pale green, are arranged in rows, like newly washed pebbles; the tiny *calamaretti, fragoline di mare*, are black and grey (cooked in a wine sauce they turn a deep pink); the rose-coloured slippery little fish called *signorini* are for the *frittura*; the *scampi* are pallid compared to the brilliant prawns; an orange *langouste* is a tamed beast beside a black lobster, lashing furiously.

Another market with its own very characteristic flavour is that of Cagliari, in the island of Sardinia. Spread out in flat baskets large as cartwheels are all the varieties of fish which go into *ziminù*, the Sardinian version of fish soup: fat, scaly little silver fish streaked with lime green; enormous octopus, blue, sepia, mauve, and turquoise, curled and coiled and petalled like some heavily embroidered marine flower; the *pescatrice* again, that ugly hooked angler fish; cold stony little clams, here called *arselle*; *tartufi di mare*; silvery slippery sardines; rose-red mullets in every possible size, some small as sprats, like doll's-house fish; the fine lobsters for which Sardinia is famous. To eat the plainly grilled or fried fish in this island is an experience from which any town dweller, accustomed to fish which must have been in the ice at least a day or two, will derive great pleasure. The mullet, the thin slices of fresh tunny, the little clams, seem to have been washed straight from the sea into the frying pan, so fresh and tender is their flesh. In such conditions there is no necessity to create complicated sauces and garnishes; and, indeed, for the cooking of fish Italian cooks are mainly content to concentrate their skill on the arts of frying, grilling, and roasting.

Summer Holidays

August rain swishes down on the leaves of the wild jungly tree which grows, rootless apparently, in the twelve inch strip of gravel outside my London kitchen. I am assured by a gardener that the plant originated in Kamchatka, but now it looks more like something transplanted from the Orinoco. Staring out at it, hunched into her bumble-bee-in-a-black-mood attitude, my cat suddenly jumps up, presses her face to the window, doesn't like what she sees, comes back, wheels round, washes her face, re-settles herself on her blanket, stares out again. I feel restless too. Remembering other rain-soaked Augusts, English holiday Augusts, I am melancholy, I have a *nostalgie de la pluie*. North Cornwall and its leafy lanes dripping, dripping; the walk in a dressing gown and gum boots through long squelching grass to the stream at the end of the field to fetch water for our breakfast coffee. At the nearest farmhouse they can let us have a pint or two of milk every day; no, not cream, and no eggs or butter, these come out on the grocery van from Penzance. Will there be any pilchards? How lovely to eat them grilled like fresh sardines, except we have only a primus in the kitchen, no grill or oven, so I don't know how we'll cook them; in the bent tin frying pan I suppose. The question never arises though, it isn't the season they say, it's too early, too late, too rough, too cold, too warm. Shopping in Penzance we run to earth what we think is a Cornish regional speciality. At Woolworths. Gingery biscuits, bent and soft, delicious, much nicer than the teeth-breaking sort. (Years later, I find tins of biscuits called Cornish Fairings at my London grocers, and buy them, hoping they are the same. They are meant to be, I think, but they are too crisp. I like the squadgy ones, I expect the recipe is secret to the Penzance Woolworths.)

In one of the grey, slatey villages – St. Just in Roseland – we buy saffron buns, dazzling yellow, only the dye doesn't seem to go quite all the way through, and I think it must be anatto not saffron, anyway there is no taste and the buns are terribly dry. Next day the children take up with a fisherman on the beach and he has given them a huge crawfish. How I wish he hadn't. We can't leave the thing clacking round on dry land. Dry – well, everything is relative.

D. says she will take the girls out for the afternoon to look for Land's End (yesterday it was curtained off by rain, she pretends to think perhaps it will be different today) and leaves me to the grisly task of cooking the crawfish. The only advantage of being the Expedition's cook is that I am entitled to stay indoors. Our largest cooking vessel is a 2-pint earthenware stew-pot, so I have to boil the lobster in the water bucket. The RSPCA pamphlet says the most humane way to cook lobsters and their like is to put them in cold water, and as it heats the animal loses consciousness and dies peacefully. I never met a fisherman or a fishmonger or a chef who paid any attention to this theory, and few who had even heard of it. I like to believe in it, and also I think that given the right conditions the system produces a better-cooked lobster, less tough than the ones plunged in boiling water, but a bucket of water takes a powerful long time to heat up on a small primus stove, and that animal would be lying in its bath for a good hour before the water boils – and suppose you have to take it off and re-charge the primus in the course of the operation?

The year after the Cornish coastguard's cottage, it is a loaned bungalow on the West Coast of Scotland. Rain drumming on the corrugated iron roof makes a stimulating background rhythm for my work on the index of a book about Italian cooking. Thank heaven for these wet Augusts. In what other climate could one do three months' work during a fortnight's holiday? *Gragnano, grancevole, grignolino, gorgonzola, granita, San Gimignano,* no, *Genoa, ginepro*. L. comes in drenched but with a fresh supply of Dainty Dinah toffees and the delicious rindless Ayrshire bacon we have discovered in the village shop, and the information that at high tide the fisherman will be at the landing stage with crabs and lobsters for sale. Must we? Lacrima Cristi, lamb, lampreys, Lambrusco, lasagne . . . All right, on with our Wellingtons and sou'westers. As it turns out the fisherman is *not* selling crabs and lobsters, nobody eats them here, nasty dirty things, they are for despatch to a fish paste factory in Yorkshire. I am relieved. Too soon. He holds out a great rogue crab. Here, take this. Sixpence. 'How shall I cook him? In boiling water or cold?'

'Boiling.'

'The RSPCA says –'

'Don't know about that –'

'– cruel –'

'Dirty beast. Let him suffer it out.'

On Tory island, off the Donegal coast – two hours off, in an open boat, on what the Irish describe as a nice soft day, the Scots as a bit mixed, and I as a hurricane, a woman tells me that the best way to cook crabs is to pull off their claws and roast them in the ashes and throw the truncated bodies back in the sea. Some evidence of this ancient folk custom was indeed around. After all perhaps I am better off not inquiring too closely into the local cookery lore of these islands. The kind of windfall cookery which comes one's way in London demands a less ferocious spirit. Rapid action is more to the point.

Pale apricot coloured chanterelle mushrooms from sodden Surrey woods have only to be washed and washed and washed until all the grit has gone, every scrap, and cooked instantly before the bloom and that extraordinary, delicate, almost flower-like scent have faded. (As L. was returning to our Scottish bungalow that other year with a damp bundle of these exquisite mushrooms gallantly gathered during a storm, the schoolmaster's wife stopped to look and used the same expression as the fisherman did about the crab – 'You're never going to eat those dirty things?' But she was a kindly woman, and the same evening invited us in for whisky which would dispel the effects of our folly.)

In contrast, a bunch of sweet basil, the kind with big fleshy floppy leaves, fills the kitchen with a quite violently rich spice smell as it is pounded up with Parmesan, garlic, olive oil and walnuts for a *pesto* sauce for pasta. Again, action has to be taken immediately. That basil was wet, and by tomorrow will have begun to turn black. The vine leaves from the wall of a house near Cambridge, now they can wait a day or two, wrapped in a food bag in the refrigerator, then they will make a lining for a pot of baked mushrooms – a recipe of Italian origin intended for big fat boletus and other wild fungi, and which, it turns out, works a notable change in cultivated mushrooms, making you almost believe you have picked them yourself in some early morning field.

The brined vine leaves in tins from Greece work perfectly in the same way too – all that is necessary before using them is a rinse in a colander under running cold water – but fresh ones, a couple of dozen or so if they are small, should be plunged into a big saucepan of boiling water. As soon as it comes back to the boil take them out, drain them, and line a shallow earthenware pot with them, keeping some for the top. Fill up with flat mushrooms, about ½ lb for two, scatter the chopped stalks on top, add salt, freshly milled pepper, several whole small cloves of garlic which don't necessarily have to be eaten but are essential to the flavour, pour in about four tablespoons of olive oil and cover with vine leaves and the lid of the pot and bake in a very moderate oven for about one hour – less or more according to the size of the mushrooms. When the vine leaves are large and tough they do their work all right but are too stringy to eat; little tender ones are delicious (not the top layer, they have dried out) and there is a good deal of richly flavoured thin dark juice; for soaking it up one needs plenty of bread.

A la marinière

Although I lived all my childhood within a few miles of the sea I don't think we ever ate shellfish at home. I don't remember ever seeing a lobster or an oyster until I was grown-up, and as for mussels, I had never heard of them, let alone tasted them, until I went to stay with a Norman family in a farmhouse at Bièville, a village near Caen.

The cooking at Bièville was done by Marie, a local girl hardly older than I was – about seventeen – and her only assistant in the kitchen was her brother, aged about eight. All our food was delicate and delicious, there was always beautiful butter and fresh bread for breakfast, and at midday simply cooked meat and a separate dish of vegetables from the farm's kitchen garden. I had become accustomed to good middle-class French cooking in the same family's Paris household, so none of these things struck me as unusual until, one day, Marie came into the dining-room bearing a big tureen of mussels, cooked in some sort of creamy sauce flecked with parsley and probably other garden herbs as well. The appearance, the smell and the taste of those mussels were to me most fascinating and mysterious. The little black-shelled objects didn't seem like fish at all, they had the same kind of magical quality as mushrooms, the real field mushrooms which, as children, we had so often brought home for breakfast after a dawn search in the fields round our home in the Sussex Downs. Maybe the cream sauce had something to do with the association of sensation, for we had had a Nannie who always used to cook our breakfast mushrooms over the nursery fire in cream, whisked away no doubt, from the kitchen regions before the cook was up and about. As in most households, Nannie and the cook thoroughly disapproved of each other, and had she known this private cookery was going on upstairs in the nursery, the cook would have made a blistering row. We must have been aware of this, as children always are of tension between grown-ups, because Nannie's mushrooms had the charm of the forbidden. We must never be caught eating them. So those Norman mussels which reminded me, for whatever reason, of our secret childhood feasts, became for ever endowed with the mystery of far-off and almost unobtainable things. And to this day the first food I ask for when I land in France is a dish of mussels. Before embarking on the ferry to return home I always try to go to a restaurant where I know there will be mussels, sweet, small mussels, so small in fact that you get about seventy or eighty to a portion, and a London housewife would be indignant if she were asked to clean so many. I have seen, in the market at Rouen, the fishwives selling mussels already cleaned in a gigantic whirling machine – but at the Restaurant La Marée, nearby in the place du Marché, I was told that the machine isn't good enough – the little things must all be cleaned by hand.

The difference between these little mussels of the Norman coast (the best are reputed to come from Yport, although I suspect that a certain quantity are brought over from the English south coast where nobody bothers about them) and the great big Dutch ones we get in London, is just the difference between the field mushrooms of my childhood and today's cultivated mushrooms – the cultivated ones are easy to get and very nice but they lack magic. But that doesn't mean you can't make very excellent dishes out of them if you treat them right, and the same applies to urban fishmongers' mussels – although I must say I try to buy small Welsh or Irish mussels whenever possible, in preference to the huge Dutch ones, which to me seem dry and savourless.

But whichever kind you have, be sure to clean them very meticulously, scraping, scrubbing, bearding and rinsing them in a great deal of cold water and discarding any that are broken or open or abnormally heavy – the latter will probably be full of mud, and one may very well spoil the entire dish.

CROÛTONS À LA MARINIÈRE

For a little first course dish for two people, clean a quart of mussels, put them in a saucepan with a teacup of water and open them over a fairly fast flame. As they open, remove them to a plate, filter the liquid through a muslin, return it to a clean pan, into it put a finely chopped shallot or clove of garlic, a couple of tablespoons of chopped parsley and a small glass of white wine.

Let this boil rapidly until reduced by half. Shell the mussels. (All this can be done in advance.)

Just before serving, fry 4 slices of French bread in butter or olive oil and put them in warmed soup plates.

Heat up the mussels in the prepared sauce – this will take just about I minute – pour the whole mixture over the croûtons and serve immediately.

Improvised Cooking for Holidays and Week-ends

The kitchens of holiday houses, whether cramped and larderless, or vast, bare, with a day's march between sink and stove, usually have a stony bleakness in common. However adequate the beds or satisfactory the view, the kitchen equipment will probably consist of a tin frying pan, a chipped enamel saucepan, one Pyrex casserole without a lid, and a rusty knife with a loose handle.

Some extra organization before setting off, a basket packed with a small supply of kitchen comforts, does much to alleviate the irritation of coping with a capricious and unfamiliar stove and the vagaries of the food supply in the country or at the seaside. A good kitchen knife and a bread knife are essential pieces of equipment (cutting sandwiches with a blunt instrument may be part of holiday routine, but is very exasperating). A food mill for making purées and mashed potatoes saves hours of time, a sieve for sauces is never to be found except in one's own kitchen; some muslin squares for draining cream cheese made from the milk which inevitably goes sour, a large thermos jar in which to store the ice which has to be begged from the local pub or fishmonger, your own potato peeler, a pepper mill – these things may be a nuisance to pack, but they will prove worth the trouble. Assuming that there will be either no oven or that if there is you will only find out how it works on the last day of your stay, it is advisable to take a heavy pan for pot roasting or slow simmering, and an asbestos mat over which it may be left on a low flame while unattended.

As well as being simple, holiday food ought to provide a change from all-the-year-round dishes; it is nice to do away with the routine roast, but without having to rely on tins. One hopes to find garden vegetables, and perhaps butter, eggs and cream; possibly there will be wild rabbits, and river fish, there might even be fish from the sea (the best lobsters and crabs I have ever eaten were bought from fishermen during seaside holidays, carried home with their angry claws tied up in a handkerchief, and dropped thankfully into a pot or bucket filled with boiling water, and eaten with butter and salt).

Village shops, however, will not provide imported cheeses or sausages; so it is worth while taking a small supply of Parmesan or Gruyère cheese, some tins of Frankfurter sausages, wine for cooking (cheap wine is generally only to be found in large towns). Olive oil is another essential supply, or you will have to buy it at considerable expense in medicine bottles from the local chemist. Some good pasta or rice will provide substantial dishes for hungry walkers and swimmers, and since people on holiday usually demand large breakfasts see that there is a good pan for fried eggs and bacon and potatoes. Cheap pans which blacken and burn make for hard work and bad temper.

Marketing and preparing for three or four meals at a time is an obvious necessity at holiday time, and the following few recipes may provide ideas for people who like to provide their family and friends with nice food even though it has to be improvised, but who obviously don't want to spend all day grappling with an inadequate stove, cold washing-up water, and dented saucepans in which the food sticks in the middle while it remains quite uncooked round the edges.

RABBIT IN WHITE WINE

Three dishes can be made from one large rabbit or two smaller ones with very little work.

Keeping the hind legs separate, cut the rest of the rabbit into 6 or 8 pieces. Season them well with salt, pepper, lemon juice and plenty of thyme. Into a casserole, with a little dripping put a quarter pound of bacon cut into squares; let it melt a little; add the pieces of rabbit and let them brown on each side. In another saucepan bring half a tumbler of white wine to the boil, set light to it, and when it has finished burning pour it over the rabbit. This process reduces the wine and will give body and flavour to the sauce. (If you happen to be in the cider country use draught cider instead of white wine; in which case simply heat it up before pouring it over the rabbit.) Add hot water to come just level with the pieces of rabbit, cover the pan and let it simmer about an hour. Have ready in a bowl the liver of the rabbit pounded with a clove of garlic, a handful of chopped parsley and one of breadcrumbs. At the last minute add this mixture to the sauce, stirring over the lowest possible flame for a minute or two. The sauce will thicken, but if it boils again the liver will separate into tiny particles, which will not affect the taste of the dish but will take away from its appearance. Should mushrooms be available add half a pound of them, sliced, to the dish ten minutes before finishing the sauce. Tomatoes, fried, grilled or à la Provençale (stuffed with parsley and garlic), go well with rabbit; and so do sauté potatoes.

RABBIT PÂTÉ

Put the two legs of the rabbit which you have kept aside into a pan with a tumbler of white wine or cider. Cook them for 20 minutes and when it has cooled take the meat from the bones (the orthodox way of preparing pâté is to take the meat off the bones before it is cooked, a method which makes a good deal of hard work). Cut a few of the best pieces into small fillets and put the rest through a mincer, or chop it finely. Add 4 or 5 rashers of bacon, also chopped, and the contents of a small tin of liver or pork pâté; season the mixture rather highly with ground black pepper, a little grated lemon peel, thyme, garlic and a scraping of nutmeg; arrange the minced mixture and the little fillets in layers in any small receptacle which can be used for steaming – a pudding basin will do if there is no earthenware terrine, or one of those aluminium tins with a close covering lid which are sold in camping equipment shops; moisten the pâté with some of the liquid in which the legs of the rabbit were originally cooked, preferably reduced by 10 minutes' fast boiling. Cover the pâte with greaseproof paper and steam for half an hour. (Pâtés are usually steamed in the oven, but the top of the stove is quite satisfactory.) When it has cooled pour over it a layer of melted dripping, which will seal it, so that it can be kept for several days; it will be excellent with toast, taken as it is on a picnic, or made into sandwiches.

RABBIT AND LEMON SOUP

Out of the bones of the rabbit and the usual soup vegetables, herbs and seasonings make a stock; it will not be very strong, but it doesn't matter. Add any of the sauce which happens to be left over from the original rabbit dish. Strain the stock and in it boil 2 tablespoons of rice; have ready in a bowl 2 eggs beaten up with the juice of a lemon. Pour some of the soup over this, stirring hard, then return the mixture to the pan, letting it reheat a minute or two without boiling. This soup, although it has not such a fine flavour, is similar to the Greek *Avgolémono* which is made with chicken stock.

BŒUF EN DAUBE

This is another way of making three dishes with one batch of ingredients. 3½ to 4 lb. of stewing beef in one piece, 1 lb. of carrots, garlic, onions and a calf's or pig's foot, thyme, bayleaves and red or white wine are the necessities. Make a few holes in the beef with a small knife and in these put some half cloves of garlic. Rub the beef all over with salt, pepper and fresh thyme. Brown the meat on both sides in a little dripping; pour over a tumbler of wine and when it bubbles set light to it. Keep it boiling until the flames die down. Remove the meat and wine to a capacious casserole; add a sliced onion, the split calf's foot and the carrots, plus a couple of bayleaves and another branch of thyme. Cover the meat with hot water, set the pan on a very low flame and cook it until the meat is absolutely tender; it may take anything from four to six hours, according to the toughness or otherwise of the meat. This part of the cooking can be done regardless of the time you are going to dine; the daube can be strained, left to cool, the fat skimmed off, and reheated gently, or it can be served as soon as it is cooked. In any case put the hot beef on to a serving dish with the carrots and only a small portion of the gravy. With it serve either a bowl of well-buttered *pasta* or mashed potatoes, to soak up the juice of the meat. For the next day's meal put what is left of the beef into a bowl; over it pour the liquid which you have reserved, which will set to a jelly. With a small spoon dipped in a bowl of hot water skim off the fat, and your dish is ready to serve. Potatoes, baked or boiled in their jackets, a fresh garden lettuce, a salad of finely sliced raw cabbage, a rice and tomato salad, almost anything except brussels sprouts will go with it.

In the meantime, with the calf's or pig's foot which you have kept aside make a second lot of stock; add some more onions, carrots and herbs and 2 pints of hot water; simmer it for about an hour, and strain it. With this any number of soups can be devised but one of the most successful is an improvised onion soup.

ONION SOUP

For four people slice six large onions very thinly; on this depends the success of the soup. In your casserole melt two tablespoons of beef dripping; cook the onions in this, stirring fairly often so that they turn gently brown without getting crisp, and finally form an almost amalgamated mass; season with salt and pepper, and pour over the heated stock, adding water if there is not quite enough. Cook for another 10 to 15 minutes; always supposing there is no oven or grill with which to *gratiner* the soup, prepare a thick slice of toast for each person, lightly buttered and spread with grated cheese. Place each one in a soup plate and ladle the onion soup over it.

SHELLFISH RISOTTO

Not quite the orthodox risotto but excellent, and simple. For four people you will need a small lobster or two crawfish (langouste) tails, or 2 dozen prawns, which should have been cooked in a court-bouillon of white wine, water, an onion, and herbs. Leave them to cool in the liquid, and then take them out of their shells. If lobster or crawfish cut them into dice; if prawns cut each in half.

In a fireproof shallow casserole or braising pan melt 2 oz. of butter. In this fry a sliced onion until it is golden. Put in the rice (two tea-cupsful) and stir round until the butter is all absorbed; pour over boiling water to cover the rice; you will have to stir it from time to time, but not continuously. When the first lot of water is absorbed add more until the rice is all but cooked; now add about a breakfast cup of the stock in which the fish was cooked; three minutes before serving stir in the shell fish, two tablespoons of grated Parmesan and a good lump of butter. Serve more cheese separately.

The risotto will take approximately 40 minutes to

cook, and for the last 10 minutes it must be stirred constantly.

CHAFING DISH LOBSTER

Olive oil, spring onions, tomatoes, sherry, marsala or white wine or vermouth, lemon, salt and pepper, a cooked lobster.

Warm 3 tablespoons of olive oil in a chafing dish or sauté pan. Put in the bulbous part of 6 to 8 spring onions, whole. Let them melt a minute, add two quartered tomatoes (skinned if possible), salt and pepper, let them cook 2 minutes; pour over a small glass of the sherry, marsala, white wine or vermouth (white wine or vermouth are best). Let it bubble. Add the lobster meat cut into squares and let it heat through gently.

Squeeze a little lemon juice over, and sprinkle with a little of the green part of the spring onions.

PRAWNS ON THE GRASS

1 lb. of spinach, 2 hard-boiled eggs, 4 oz. of peeled prawns, 3 to 4 oz. cream, salt, pepper, nutmeg, butter.

Cook the cleaned spinach, drain, squeeze dry in your hands and chop it, not too finely. Melt a little butter (about 1 oz.) in a chafing dish or sauté pan, heat the spinach, season it with salt, pepper and nutmeg. Put the prawns and the sliced eggs on top and pour the cream over. Cover the pan and simmer gently for 3 to 4 minutes.

MOULES AU GRATIN

Mussels are not generally obtainable in England during the summer months, but for those people who may find themselves in perhaps a holiday house in France or the Mediterranean, where mussels are eaten all the year round, I include this one recipe, which is one of the best of mussel dishes.

Open the mussels over the fire in a heavy pan, in their own liquid. When they have cooled shell them, and put two mussels into the half-shells. Arrange them in a fireproof dish, and pour melted butter or olive oil over them, then a light sprinkling of breadcrumbs mixed with an equal quantity of Parmesan cheese, a little chopped parsley and garlic, and pepper. Pour over a little of the strained juice from the mussels and put into a moderate oven sufficiently long for them to get hot. Serve quickly, with lemon.

When mussels are to be opened over the fire, shelled, and then reheated in a sauce, take great care not to over-cook them in the first place or they will be shrivelled and tough.

COLD OMELETTE

Make a plain omelette with three or four eggs; instead of folding it slide it out flat on to a plate. When it is cold garnish it with a purée made from cold chicken and ham or with the rabbit pâté already described, in fact with any cold meat mixture as long as it is not too liquid. Roll the omelette as you would a pancake.

MUSHROOMS

I have no advice to offer as to the safety or otherwise of eating unfamiliar fungi. My own knowledge of the subject is limited to personal experiment, from which I have so far emerged unscathed; I have only two or three recipes to give for those people who are sure enough of their knowledge or judgement to cook and eat those fungi which they find in the woods or fields. There are only three deadly fungi, and one of these, the Amanita Printania, superficially resembles the common field mushroom. This may account for the fact that in Italy, where all kinds of fungi which would terrify English people are constantly eaten, the ordinary field mushroom is very rarely picked.

On the west coast of Scotland I have, to the horror and disgust of the inhabitants, cooked and eaten several different fungi. The best of these were the apricot-coloured, trumpet-shaped cantharellus. They need plenty of washing and if they are large they should be cut into strips (the small ones are the best). They should be stewed gently in oil for 15 or 20 minutes (longer if they are large ones), with the addition at the last minutes of a little garlic, parsley and breadcrumbs (to absorb the oil), salt and pepper. Strips of ham or bacon can be added, and they can be used as a filling for omelettes, or piled on top of scrambled eggs; in France and Italy they are fairly commonly eaten, either as a separate dish or an accompaniment to chicken, or in a risotto.

BOLETUS

Boletus edulis, the *cèpes* of France, are quite common in English woods and forests. They are delicious when absolutely fresh, but very quickly go sodden and rotten. The stalks are tough and should be chopped finely; *Boletus* are best stewed in oil, for about 40 minutes, with the addition of chopped shallots, garlic and parsley. There is also an excellent way of stuffing and baking them; prepare a finely chopped mixture of ham or bacon, garlic, breadcrumbs, a very little Parmesan cheese and the chopped stalks. Put a tablespoon of the stuffing in each *cèpe*, fill them up with oil and bake them in a slow oven, in a covered dish, for about an hour. From time to time add a little more oil.

FIELD MUSHROOMS

To grill field mushrooms wash them, remove the stalks and marinade them for an hour in olive oil flavoured with salt and pepper and a little fresh thyme. Put them under the grill with a little of the oil, and cook them fairly fast, turning them over and over so they do not dry up. The large flat field mushrooms are also delicious fried, preferably I think in bacon or pork fat, rather than butter. Don't let the fat get too hot before putting in the mushrooms, and when they appear to have absorbed it all, turn the heat down, and in a minute or two the mushrooms start to yield their juice. Continue cooking them gently, sprinkling them with salt and pepper. They should be cooked skin side down and need not be turned over. Eat them with fried bread.

MUSHROOMS COOKED IN CREAM

To make a really good dish of mushrooms in cream very fresh little button mushrooms from the field are needed.

Clean them (say ½ lb.) with a damp cloth and do not peel them. Bring a coffee-cupful of water to the boil and squeeze in a little lemon juice and a pinch of salt. Put in the mushrooms and let them cook about 2 minutes. Strain them.

The sauce is prepared by stirring 2 or 3 teaspoons of flour into ¼ pint of cream. Bring to the boil and when the sauce has thickened put in the strained mushrooms and cook another 5 minutes, adding ground black pepper and more salt if necessary.

POTATOES AND MUSHROOMS

When you have picked only a few mushrooms, not enough to make a whole dish of them, try this mixture of mushrooms and potatoes.

1 lb. of potatoes, ½ lb. of mushrooms, 1 oz. of butter, a clove of garlic, a small onion, olive oil, the juice of half a lemon, parsley.

Cut the peeled potatoes into thin slices. Heat the oil and butter in an earthenware pan and sauté the chopped onion. Add the garlic, then the potatoes. Simmer for 10 minutes then put in the cleaned and sliced mushrooms, and barely cover with water. Season with salt and pepper, cover the pan, and cook on a moderate flame until the potatoes are tender. Add a little chopped parsley and the lemon juice, and serve in the pan in which it has cooked.

Two or three fillets of anchovies can be added at the same time as the mushrooms.

PIGEONS STEWED WITH LETTUCES

Pigeons are often tough little birds, but in the country there are often a great many to be disposed of. A pigeon gives an excellent flavour if cooked with the meat and vegetables for a broth; with three pigeons a very nice little terrine or pâté, enough for about 8 people, can be made. Baby pigeons are very good split in half and grilled. Older birds make a good country dish cooked in the following way with lettuces.

For each pigeon you need two cos lettuces, a cupful of meat or chicken stock, a rasher of bacon and some parsley, shallots, herbs and the usual seasonings. First blanch the pigeons in boiling water for 5 minutes and cut them in half. Then blanch the lettuces. Cut the lettuces down the middle, without separating the two halves; spread them with a mixture of chopped shallots, parsley, herbs, salt and pepper. Put half a pigeon in the middle, tie them up, and place them in a pan lined with the bacon rashers; pour the stock over them and simmer gently for about an hour and a half; put them in the serving dish, thicken the sauce with a yolk of egg, squeeze in a little lemon juice and pour over the pigeons.

ROASTED CHEESE

This is not a particularly summery dish, but is so quick and easy to make, and provides such a good meal in a hurry, and for people who live alone, that it is worth knowing. The best cheeses to use for it are Cheddar, Gruyère, Emmenthal, or Bel Paese.

Cut 6 or 7 slices from a French loaf, each about ¼ inch thick. Cut the same number of slices of cheese, a little thinner. Cover each slice of bread with a slice of cheese and arrange them in a long fireproof dish (or baking tin if you are making a quantity) and put them in the top of a very hot oven (Regulo 8). In 8 to 10 minutes the dish will be ready, the cheese melting and the bread just getting crisp. Before eating the croûtons sprinkle them plentifully with freshly ground black pepper, or if you like, with a tomato sauce made as follows:

For the amount given, melt two chopped ripe tomatoes in butter, add salt, pepper, a scrap of garlic, and a little chopped parsley, or any other herb you like. Cook for about 3 minutes only. Pour over the cheese as soon as the dish is taken out of the oven.

BAKED CHEESE SANDWICHES

Butter thin slices of brown bread (best if two or even three days old), make them into sandwiches with a filling of thickish slices of Cheddar or Double Gloucester cheese, seasoned with freshly milled black pepper and a little mustard.

Arrange the sandwiches in a baking dish. Sprinkle each with a few drops of vinegar (this is important), press the bread well down, bake the sandwiches for 15 to 20 minutes in the centre of a medium hot oven, gas No. 4 or 5, 350 to 375 deg. F.

When the sandwiches are ready, the bread should be crisp and the cheese filling just barely melting.

A highly useful little dish for children, for people who live alone, for those cooking under difficult conditions – and for anybody who knows nothing at all about cooking but would like a change from food out of tins and packets.

HERB CHEESE

Into ½ lb. of home-made milk cheese stir about half a teacupful of chopped fresh lemon thyme and sweet marjoram, in equal quantities, with the addition of a chopped fresh bayleaf. Season with salt and ground black pepper, pile the cheese up in a dish, and leave it several hours before serving, to give the flavour of the herbs time to penetrate the cheese. This cheese has a lovely fresh flavour. It can be eaten simply with brown bread, or, with the addition of 2 or 3 tablespoons of grated Parmesan can be stirred into a dish of hot spaghetti or noodles.

Instead of lemon thyme and marjoram, chopped borage leaves give a very delicate and unexpected flavour of cucumber to a cream cheese.